FRENCH MINOR RAILWAYS
Vol. 1

PETER SMITH

ARPAJON. - Le Tramway

COPYRIGHT 2013 PETER SMITH

ISBN-13 978-1494807085

ISBN-10 149480084

INTRODUCTION

This book illustrates seven French secondary railways, five narrow gauge and two standard gauge, in the hope that modellers may be inspired to recreate some of the wonderful scenes. There are tiny stations squeezed into the streets of towns, rural stations with hardly a house to be seen in any direction, busy lines and barely surviving lines and one line that should certainly never have been built. From that to a line that once ran right into Paris and you have a wide enough selection to tempt anyone. I won't be held responsible though….be warned, these little French railways are highly addictive!

CHAPTER 1   BARBIZON TO MELUN   Page 3

CHAPTER 2   THE ARPAJONNAIS TRAMWAY   Page 20

CHAPTER 3   THE AULT TRAMWAY   Page 46

CHAPTER 4   CHALLENS TO FROMENTINE   Page 55

CHAPTER 5   NANGIS TO JOUY LE CHATEL   Page 66

CHAPTER 6   RENNES TO PLELAN   Page 77

CHAPTER 7 ST NAZAIRE TO LA ROCHE BERNARD   Page 87

CHAPTER 1 BARBIZON TO MELUN.

The metre gauge tramway from Barbizon to Melun ran from 1899 to 1938 with a 12km route entirely within the Seine et Marne department. A second line ran from Barbizon to Milly la Foret which lies just inside Seine et Oise. The station at Barbizon was a terminus, the trains reversing there before continuing their journey..

During the late 19th century there had been many attempts to connect the towns with a railway but all had failed because the War Department were concerned that the line would be of use to an enemy intent on reaching Paris. Not until a proposal was made to build a tramway rather than a railway did things progress, an application by M. Nabias of Paris being accepted to build a metre gauge tramway. The paperwork was completed in 1897, work began in 1898 and in 1899 the line opened at which time ownership was transferred from M. Noias to the Seine et Marne Southern Tramway Company. The line to Melun opened on Sunday March 26th 1898, with commercial traffic beginning the following Wednesday. The second line to Milly opened in September 1910, taking seven years to build in contrast to the first line, so for eleven years Barbizon station was the terminus of a single route.

There were five locomotives, all Corpet Louvet 030's; three were built in 1899 and two more added when the new line was opened in 1908. They were all named after places on the route; the first three loco's were No 1 Melun, No 2 Barbizon and No 3 Milly, followed in 1908 by No 4 Chailly and No 5 Arbonne.

The line ran from Barbizon through Dammarie and Chauilly to the larger town of Melun where a connection was made with trains on the PLM line to Paris. Departures were allowed to wait for fifteen minutes if the Paris train was running late! The journey took just over an hour there were five trains a day from Barbizon and six from Melun before the war. There were eight request halts on the route as well, serving smaller places. The journey on to Paris took around 40 minutes, depending on which train was used. Another tramway ran from Melun to Verneuil, as well as Melun having an electrified town tramway; all three converged outside the PLM station.

The First World War affected the lines badly; at the armistice only two loco's were still useable. The company had debts of 140,000 francs and the lines never again made a profit.

Two four wheeled railcars were introduced in 1922 and 1924 with a third following in 1937, but by that time it was too late to save the lines.

Milly to Chailly was abandoned on July 31st 1938, the Melun section following on September 30th. The rails remained in place until 1952 when all the infrastructure was scrapped.

This is sadly a familiar story; lines built in a burst of optimism in the late 19th century, cruelly mistreated during the First World war and unable to recover in the face of rising costs and competition from road transport. Many closed in the late 1930's; few survived much beyond World War Two.

Happily the postcards take us back to that age of optimism in the early 1900's when the sun shone and everyone travelled by rail to get to work, to market or to school. This selection of postcards illustrate the line during that period; it would make a delightful model.

LIGNE DE
MELUN
A
BARBIZON
FORÊT DE
FONTAINEBLEAU
HORAIRE DES TRAINS
ALLER
STATIONS
RETOUR
STATIONS
Ste des TRAMWAYS SUD de SEINE & MARNE
Administration _ 28, Rue Dajot _ MELUN
IMP. CHARLES VERNEAU. 114 Rue Oberkampf. PARIS.

Melun tramway station with Corpet No.2 'Barbizon' standing in the station. The spark arresting chimney looks very North American. The station was in the 'Place de la Gare', the tramway approaching the town from the south and terminating at the P.L.M. station rather than crossing the river to enter the town centre.

Below is one of the other engines in the same spot, showing how tightly the line curved. The leading Fourgon appears to be in the same colours as the coaches.

5. MELUN. - GARE DU TRAMWAY DE BARBIZON

Edit. Saussier, Gare de Melun

The Fourgon is shown in brown in this lovely colour postcard, but bear in mind that the artist almost certainly never saw the real thing!

When the electric tramway was built around the streets of Melun it ran along the road on the other side of the trees making a convenient interchange.

Behind the station the large building was the inevitable 'Hotel de la Gare'. This was referring to the adjacent P.L.M. station which was rather more imposing than the tramway terminus.

713. MELUN — Hôtel de la Gare et Tramway de Barbizon

MELUN. — Place de la Gare et Chemin de fer de Barbizon. — LL.

The earlier postcard below shows the Hotel before being rebuilt and modernised.

MELUN. - Le Tramway de Barbizon

Above; horse drawn cabs wait for trade from the tramway train.

Below; the P.L.M. station with the electrified town tramway on the left.

56 MELUN. — La Gare. — Lignes de Corbeil et de Lyon. — LL.

88. MELUN — Les Quais de la Gare

85. MELUN — La Gare

A tram on the town service outside the P.L.M. station around 1910.

The station is pretty much unrecognisable now: it was opened in 1849 on the line from Paris to Lyon & Marseilles but rebuilding in 1979 and 2012 has destroyed most of the original fabric.

Running south from Melun, the line ran through the small settlement of Dammarie les Lys, which is today very much as suburb of Melun. This was the first station on the line.

In the traditional manner the line ran along the streets of the village.

221 — *Dammarie-les-Lys.* — *Rue du Tramway.*
A. Siron, phot.-édit., Barbizon (S.-et-M.).

The next station was at Chailly en Biere, the largest of the through stations on the route. The yard seems to be well stocked with wagons; the main outward traffic was agricultural produce. Although they cannot be seen in the pictures the line's loco sheds and repair shops were here, though there was also a depot at Melun.

543. CHAILLY-EN-BIÈRE — La Gare

394. - Chailly-en-Bière. - La Gare.

587. CHAILLY-EN-BIÈRE — Rue de la Garenne

6 BARBIZON. — Arrivée du Tramway de Melun. — LL.

This is Barbizon station, a tiny structure to serve as the terminus of two routes. Note the turntable in the left foreground acting as a sector plate for the loop. It looks to be an idyllic spot with the trees in full leaf and the sun shining.

691. BARBIZON — Grande rue

106. BARBIZON — Rue de Barbizon

1185. - BARBIZON. - Station du Tramway

Behind the train and station is the Hotel de la Foret, the reason for the tramway terminating at this point having run through the town.

1185. - BARBIZON. - Station du Tramway

1184. - BARBIZON. - L'Entrée par Chailly

BARBIZON. — Point terminus du Tramway et Hôtel de la Forêt.

139. - BARBIZON. - Gare du Tramway

693. BARBIZON — Entrée du Village

106. BARBIZON — Grande Rue

These two pictures sum up French narrow gauge for me; the rails and the train are so much part of everyday life that no one takes the slightest notice of them……..and then one day of course, they were gone.

682. DAMMARIE-LES-LYS — Avenue de Dammarie

CHAPTER 2   THE ARPAJONNAIS TRAMWAY

Not many of us associate steam tramways with Paris, but here is one that ran right into the big city! It terminated at the town of Arpajon, a 37km run from the city terminus at the Port d'Orleans. The line ran from 1893 to 1937, when buses took over the passenger services. This was a standard gauge line, but as it has so many characteristics of the narrow gauge I hope I will be forgiven!

This was the sequence of construction:

April 27th 1893: Porte d'Orléans to Pont d'Antony

August 15th 1893: Antony in Longjumeau

February 5, 1894: Longjumeau to Montlhery

1 st May 1894: Montlhery Arpajon with a branch to Montlhery Marcoussis

10 May 1894 : The official inauguration.

The line was operated with Bicabine locomotives, but soon there was a problem. In February 1895 the City of Paris banned steam traction on tramways within the city boundaries so between Pont d'Anthony and the Porte d'Orleans compressed air power was used briefly and then electric traction powered by batteries. In 1901 the section was electrified with overhead wires, making Pont d'Anthony a transfer point for passengers.

In 1930 the electrified line was extended by 1km to Petit Massey becoming line 88a with newly introduced electric trams.

The steam worked section was looking increasingly dated and the inevitable end came in 1937 when buses took over the passenger services.

The line began at the Porte d'Orleans where there was reversing loop and a line to workshops at Montrouge. The line ran through Petit Massey, crossing from Seine into Seine et Oise. There were stations at Anthony, Morangis, Wissous, Chilly-Mazarin, Longjumeau, Ballainvilliers, Montlhery, Linas and Arpajon. In 1911 the line was extended in Arpajon to the PO station.

The line opened with a fleet of Tubize 030 bicabine locomotives which continued in use on the country section until it closed.

In the city, in 1895 compressed air locomotives from Mekarski were used until the 1901 overhead electrification when bogie tramcars were introduced. The speed limit was 12km per hour in the city and 20 kph beyond there.

43. Arpajon — Gare du Tramway

The terminus at Arpajon, with a train of four wheeled coaches alongside the road. One of them has been given an upper deck to increase capacity which looks decidedly precarious! None of the pictures show more than one coach in a train with the upper deck so there may only have been one, which may indicate how popular it was with the public.

The facilities consisted of a small station building and a separate house for the station master. In the upper picture the wooden goods shed can be glimpsed on the right.

Although it was standard gauge the line has all the charm of the narrow gauge.

Gare du Tramway

These two pictures show the goods yard and the locomotive sheds on the right.

14. ARPAJON — Station des Tramways C. L. C.

ARPAJON. - Le Tramway

High Summer at Arpajon—what a wonderful picture.

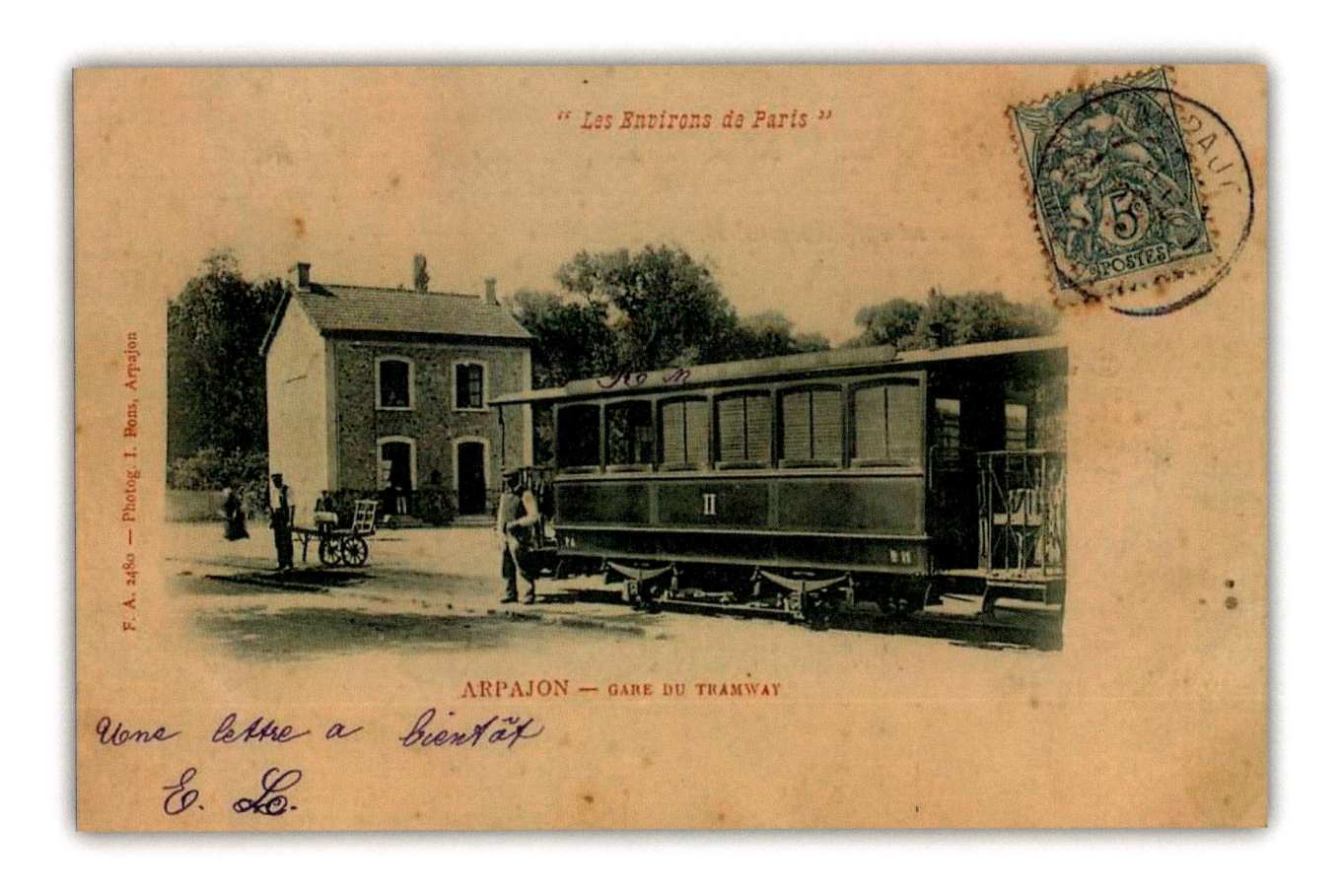

"Les Environs de Paris"

ARPAJON — GARE DU TRAMWAY

Une lettre a bientôt
E. Le.

43. Arpajon — Gare du Tramway

The following pictures show the intermediate stations in order, beginning with Linas. The halt shown below was not the main station.

LINAS — ARRÊT DU TRAMWAY

Vente exclusive, E. Laboure, à Linas

LINAS – Station du Tramway

At Montlhery the station was just a paved area in the middle of the road; this was a junction, a branch line running to Marcoussis. The train below is taking the branch line.

14 – Montlhéry (S.-et-O.) - Station du Tramway - Départ du Train de Marcoussis

13. MONTLHÉRY — Station du Tramway   C. L. C.

Montlhéry — Station du Tramway — Arrivée du Train

MONTLHÉRY. — Arrivée du Tramway.

Edition Bachot, 10, place du Marché, Montlhéry

Montlhéry. — Station du Tramway

This is the branch line terminus at Marcoussis.

MARCOUSSIS — LA GARE DU TRAMWAY

It seems sensible to take the short diversion along the branch; this is the terminus station at Marcoussis, right in the middle of town and on a very confined site—perfect for modelling.

MARCOUSSIS. - La Gare du Tramway

77. MARCOUSSIS (S.-et-O.)
Place de l'Eglise et station du Tramway

Coll. Paul Allorge, Montlhéry, série Rl 10

Approaching the station…along the main street, naturally.

That's the station on the left, right alongside the church!

Back on the main line, the next town was Ballainvilliers.

The attractive stone built station building at Longjumeau was what first attracted me to the line.

Longjumeau — Gare du Tramway

Longjumeau — Station du Tramway à Vapeur

1343. - LONGJUMEAU. - Gare du Tramway

Longjumeau — Place du Marché et Rue de Chilly

The tramway bridge over the river Yvette—it seems an odd choice for a postcard but it does make a nice picture.

The next station was Morangis—what a superb study of the train in the top picture. These don't appear to be of the same station so there may well have been two halts serving the town.

The next station was Wissous, with another of the attractive stone station buildings. The town was also served by a station on the PO railway.

Wissous – La Gare

21. WISSOUS (S.-et-O.) — La Gare du Chemin de fer sur route, de Paris à Arpajon
1re Station dans le département de Seine-et-Oise

ANTONY. — La Station des Trams

The end of the steam worked section after 1895 was Pont d'Anthony, seen here with the electric tramway on the left and a train for Arpajon ready to leave. The attractive little wooden shelter stood between the two routes.

13 - Antony
Station des Tramways

ANTONY. — La Route d'Orléans

The train seems to have backed down the line towards Paris, under the wires; perhaps the photographer thought it made a better picture!

1. ANTONY — Station du Tramway

One of the 1901 tramcars that ran into the city of Paris.

To complete the set, this is the Porte d'Orleans where the electric trams terminated and reversed on a loop line. The steam service ran to here for the first few months after the line opened.

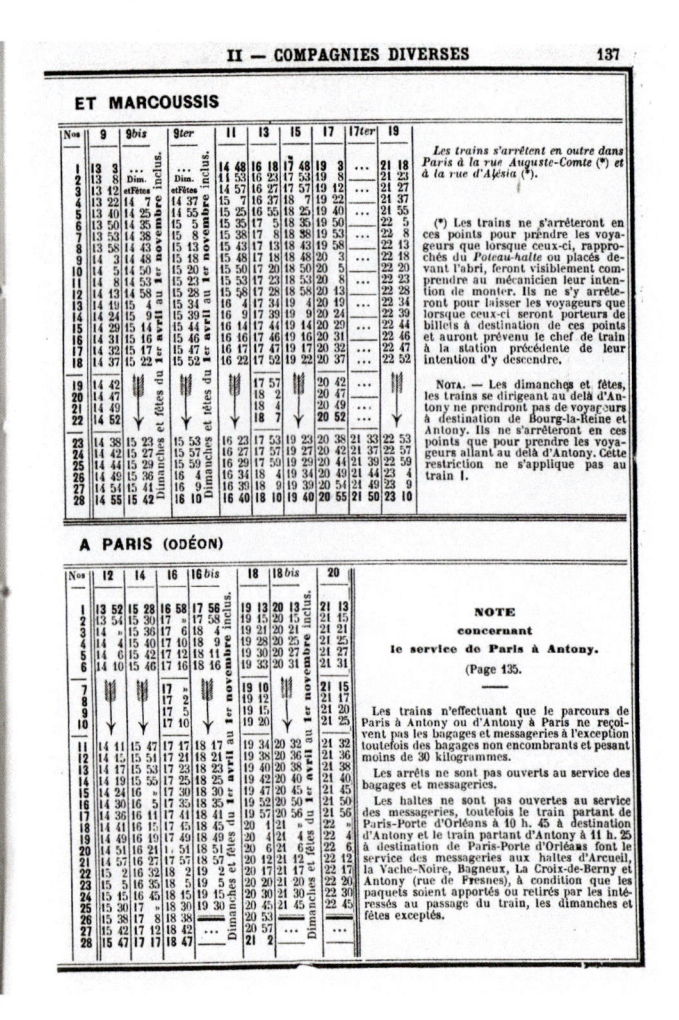

Cie du Chemin de Fer sur route — Paris-Porte-d'Orléans à Arpajon

ALLER	1	3	31 DF	5	5 M S	51 DF	53 DF	55 DF	57 DF	7	71 DF	73 DF	9	91 DF	93 DF	95 DF	11	111 DF	43
Paris-Pte-d'Orléans	6 15	6 40	7 23	8 »		8 30	9 »	9 30	9 45	10 »	10 30	11 15	12 30	13 15	13 45	14 15	14 30	15 15	16 »
Bourg-la-Reine	6 33	7 03	7 43	8 18		8 48	9 18	9 48	10 03	10 18	10 48	11 33	12 48	13 33	14 03	14 33	14 48	15 33	16 18
Pont-d'Antony	6 43	7 13	7 53	8 28		8 58	9 28	9 58	10 13	10 28	10 58	11 43	12 58	13 43	14 13	14 43	14 58	15 43	16 28
Le Petit-Massy	6 46	7 16	7 56	8 31		9 01	9 31	10 01	10 16	10 31	11 01	11 46	13 01	13 46	14 16	14 46	15 01	15 46	16 31
Wissous	6 51	7 21	8 01	8 36		9 07	9 38	10 06	10 21	10 36	11 07	11 51	13 06	13 54	14 22	14 51	15 06	15 51	16 36
Morangis	6 56	7 26	8 06	8 41		9 12	9 43	10 11	10 26	10 41	11 12	11 56	13 11	13 56	14 27	14 56	15 11	15 56	16 41
Chilly-Mazarin	6 58	7 28	8 08	8 43		9 14	9 45	10 13	10 28	10 43	11 14	11 58	13 13	13 58	14 29	14 58	15 13	15 58	16 43
Chilly-Gde-Ceinre	7 01	7 31	8 11	8 46		9 17	9 48	10 16	10 31	10 46	11 17	12 01	13 16	14 01	14 32	15 01	15 16	16 01	16 46
Longjumeau	7 06	7 35	8 16	8 51		9 21	9 53	10 20	10 36	10 51	11 22	12 06	13 21	14 06	14 37	15 06	15 21	16 06	16 51
Saulx-l.-Chartreux	7 12		8 22	8 57			9 59		10 42	10 57	11 28	12 12	13 27	14 12	14 43	15 12	15 27	16 12	16 57
Ballainvilliers	7 17			9 02			10 04			11 »	11 33	12 17	13 32	14 17		15 17	15 32	16 17	17 02
La Gge-aux-Cercles	7 22			9 07			10 09			11 07	11 38	12 22	13 37	14 22		15 22	15 37	16 22	17 07
La Ville-du-Bois	7 24			9 09			10 11			11 09	11 40	12 24	13 39	14 24		15 24	15 39	16 24	17 09
Longpont	7 25			9 10			10 12			11 10	11 41	12 25	13 40	14 25		15 25	15 40	16 25	17 10
Montlhéry arr.	7 29			9 14			10 16			11 14	11 45	12 29	13 44	14 29		15 29	15 44	16 29	17 14
— R.-St-Merry	7 34			9 19	9 24					11 19		12 34	13 49	14 34		15 49	16 34		
Linas (station)	7 36			9 21	9 26					11 21		12 36	13 51	14 36		15 51	16 36		
Leuville	7 41			9 26	9 31					11 26		12 41	13 56	14 41		15 56	16 41		
St Germain-l-Nor	7 46			9 31	9 36					11 31		12 46	14 01	14 46		16 01	16 46		
Arpajon dép.	7 47			9 32	9 37					11 32		12 47	14 02	14 47		16 02	16 47		

* Arrêt facultatif. — DF. Dimanches et Fêtes.

Embranchement de Montlhéry à Marcoussis

STATIONS									DF		
Montlhéry	6 15	7 35	9 20	11 20	13 50	15 50	17 26	18 35	19 20	20 20	
Le Houssay	6 19	7 39	9 24	11 24	13 54	15 54	17 30	18 39	19 24	20 24	
La Guillère	6 21	7 41	9 26	11 26	13 56	15 56	17 32	18 44	19 26	20 26	
Marcoussis	6 27	7 47	9 32	11 32	14 02	16 02	17 38	18 47	19 32	20 32	

Cie du Chemin de Fer sur route — Paris-Porte-d'Orléans à Arpajon (Aller) suite

ALLER	15	17	19	19 M DF	21	21 M S	23
Paris-Pte-d'Orléans	17 15	18 »	18 45		19 45		21 »
Bourg-la-Reine	17 33	18 18	19 03		20 03		21 18
Pont-d'Antony	17 43	18 28	19 13		20 13		21 28
Le Petit-Massy	17 46	18 31	19 16		20 16		21 31
Wissous	17 51	18 36	19 21		20 21		21 36
Morangis	17 56	18 41	19 26		20 26		21 41
Chilly-Mazarin	17 58	18 43	19 28		20 28		21 43
Chilly-Gde-Ceinre	18 01	18 46	19 31		20 31		21 46
Longjumeau	18 06	18 51	19 36		20 36		21 51
Saulx-l.-Chartreux	18 12	18 57	19 42		20 42		21 57
Ballainvilliers	18 17	19 02	19 47		20 47		22 02
La Gge-aux-Cercles	18 22	19 07	19 52		20 52		22 07
La Ville-du-Bois	18 24	19 09	19 54		20 54		22 09
Longpont	18 25	19 10	19 55		20 55		22 10
Montlhéry arr.	18 29	19 14	19 59		20 59		22 14
— R.-St-Merry	18 34	19 19	20 04	20 39	21 04	21 34	22 19
Linas (station)	18 36	19 21	20 06	20 41	21 06	21 36	22 21
Leuville	18 41	19 26	20 11	20 46	21 11	21 41	22 26
St-Germain-l-Nor	18 46	19 31	20 16	20 51	21 16	21 46	22 31
Arpajon dép	18 47	19 32	20 17	20 52	21 17	21 47	22 32

Les dimanches et fêtes, les trains se dirigeant au delà d'Antony ne prennent pas de voyageurs à destination de Bourg-la-Reine et Antony, ils ne s'arrêtent en ces points que pour prendre des voyag. allant au delà d'Antony. Cette restriction ne s'applique pas au train 1.

CHAPTER 3   THE AULT TRAMWAY.

The village of Ault lies on the coast of Picardy north of Le Treport and it's an attractive place, quiet and far from the pressures of modern life. That was even more the case in 1904, when it was proposed to connect Ault to the outside world by way of a tramway. It would bring development, business, prosperity, tourists, day trippers….the possibilities were endless!

As it turned out, this was possibly among the most calamitous investments in a railway in the whole of France.

The population of Ault was only 1941 in 2006; a century earlier it was even less. It was isolated, little known and economically stagnating. The community managed to raise 25,000 francs and work began on building a standard gauge tramway 12km long to a junction with the Ouest main line at Feuquieres-Fressenneville. A narrow gauge line would have been cheaper to build and to operate but the reason for standard gauge may have hinged on the possibility of through trains running from further afield. Such optimism!

The company was called the' Societe des Chemins de Fer Industrieles et Balneaire de la Somme', a title almost as long as the tramway…..it summed up the hoped for traffic, industry and the seaside. The main local industry was high quality metalworking which was anxious for an outlet for the finished products.

Authorised on 15th December 1904 construction took less than twelve months, the line opening on 24th November 1905, hardly the time of year to encourage excursion or holiday traffic. The terminus station was high above Ault, an all wooden affair with an enclosed train shed which was probably a good thing in November. There were intermediate stations at Freville-Escarbotin, Bethencourt and Tully, none of them likely to be major sources of revenue. The single line ran on fairly easy gradients, in the French tradition following the routes of existing roads for the most part. The journey took between 44 minutes and 1 hour 6 minutes, no doubt depending on whether any shunting was required or how heavy the train was. 1 hour 6 minutes for a journey of only 12km is not very fast, in fact an average speed not much more than walking pace.

Hopes rested on the following Summer season, but sadly during the winter things went from bad to worse….one train took 22 hours to complete the journey, arriving at 4am due to heavy snow. By the time the weather improved the line was already struggling to survive; pictures show a steam train but also what seems to be an early internal combustion railcar, no doubt in an effort to reduce running costs. It didn't help; the service was suspended on 31st August 1906, never to be reinstated. The line had been open for just ten months.

The line lay moribund until 1921 when the company was bought by the Society General de Chemin de fer Economiques (SE). They built a totally new line, again standard gauge, from the slightly closer junction station of Woicourt using some of the original trackbed as it got nearer to Ault. The new line was 12km long and was extended by 1km to the Phare d'Onival in 1922. The line operated until the outbreak of World War 2 when the 1km extension closed at once; the remainder was operated by the German army to bring in supplies for constructing the Atlantic Wall and a new metre gauge line ran north to connect with the Baie de Somme system. A huge quarry exploited the local 'gallets' which were used in making concrete.

It is possible that the postcards showing the brick built stations and the railcar date from the second line with the original tramway always being steam worked, but I don't think so; they look pre-WW1 to me.

The second Ault station was demolished as it was in the way of a new gun battery; as soon as the Germans left the line was abandoned, never to reopen, with official closure in 1946.

Ault was to remain a little known, picturesque village undiscovered by the tourist hordes, and today is probably the better for it. As for the original tramway, it really was not a good use of 25,000 francs!

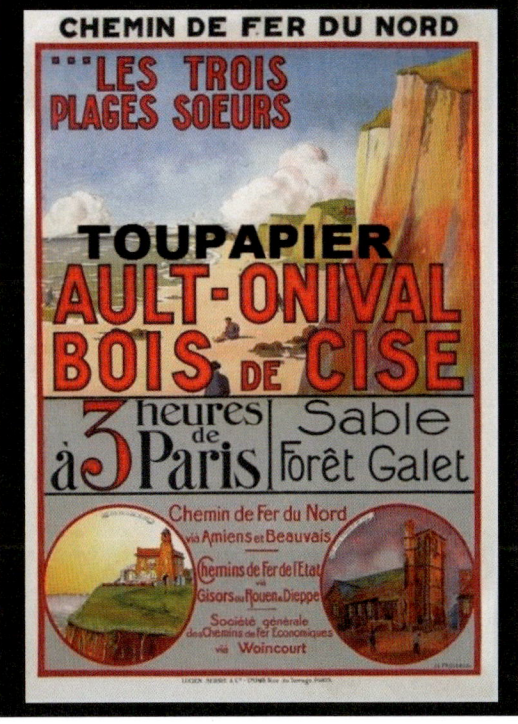

No one could accuse the main line railways of not trying to publicise the area, but to little effect.

Ault-Onival. — La Gare.

Perched on a bleak cliff top this was Ault station, a wooden construction offering welcome protection in that exposed position.

The lower picture is the best illustration I have seen of the rolling stock, very much aimed towards the potential tourist traffic. The loco is a Bicabine with side skirts; there are two pictures showing steam trains and each one has a different engine. With the railcar as well you wonder if they were just borrowing whatever was available.

AULT-ONIVAL — La Gare

48

This is the sort of scene the promoters were hoping for.

The picture below shows that the walk from the beach to the station would have been an invigorating one.

The two intermediate stations on the tramway, showing above the petrol railcar and below the steam train with a very un-French looking 020 saddle tank loco with wooden blocks for buffers in the manner of an industrial engine.

The petrol railcar running along the street in Friaucourt.

Presumably this brickworks would have been a potential source of traffic, though in practice they seem to have been very much focussed on passengers rather than freight.

The track ran through the streets of Fressenneville in the manner of a narrow gauge line.

Below is the main line station, possibly before the tramway opened.

FRESSENNEVILLE. — La Gare

A much later view of the station; the metal nameboard is interesting.

Eversam ville

CHAPTER 4 THE CHALLENS—FROMENTINE TRAMWAY

This metre gauge tramway ran for 24km from Challens to Fromentine in the Vendee region, starting life as the CdF Challens Fromentine in 1896. As was so often the case it was promoted by local people, in this case M Bley and M. Aubert.

Initial optimism not having been bourne out by actual traffic levels, the line was bought by the Depatement in 1914 and became part of the Vendee narrow gauge system in 1923. The inevitable closure came on October 1st 1949.

The route passed through the stations of Challans, Challans Ville, Sallertaine, Saint Gervias, Beauvoir sur Mer, La Barre de Monts and Fromentine.

The line opened with three Corpet Louvet 030 locomotives;

1 Corpet-Louvet , No. 614, September 7, 1895, "Challans

2 Corpet-Louvet , No. 615, December 17, 1895, "Beauvoir"

3 Corpet-Louvet , No. 616, December 30, 1895, "Fromentine".

The body of a 1st/2nd class coach built in Mans has been preserved and restored on a new underframe.

55

The main line station at Challans opened on 30th December 1878 and remains open today, on the line between Nantes and la Roche sur Yon. The tramway began here in the station forecourt.

The line began at the Etat main line station but there was a further stop at Challans Ville.

Vendée. - CHALLANS. - Hôtel de la Gare M. BELET

16. - VENDÉE. - CHALLANS. - Route de Beauvoir - Arrivée du Train de Fromentine - Le Calvaire

LA BARRE-de-MONTS (Vendée) - La Gare

The only intermediate station of which I have been able to find pictures is La Barre de Monts, a bleak and open place.

The two story part of the station building is the goods shed, with the passenger accommodation beyond. The metal box is a wagon weighbridge.

LA BARRE-de-MONTS (Vendée)
L'Océan vers Noirmoutier à
la gare de Fromentine
L. V. p.

2 - La BARRE-de-MONTS (Vendée). — Avenue de la Gare

Two pictures in high Summer; you have to look very closely to see the track disappearing in the long grass to the right of the road in the top picture. In the lower one it is a bit more evident.

5. La Barre-de-Monts (Vendée) — La mairie et la route de la gare

FROMENTINE (Vendée) - La Gare

The terminus at Fromentine; the locomotive shed can just be seen to the right of the train.

The lower picture shows the simple track plan with the station building on the right behind the train.

Fromentine (Vendée) - Arrivée du Tramway à vapeur de Challans

FROMENTINE (Vendée) — La Gare. L'arrivée d'un train

The Corpet Louvet loco is lettered 'CF' on the buffer beam so the picture was taken before 1914.

50 - FROMENTINE (Vendée). — L'Avenue de la Gare

Arrivée du train à FROMENTINE

Edition Tulasne

The wooden structure behind the station is interesting, but I have no idea what it is.

The lower view is much later, probably from the 1940's; there is a railcar in the station.

128. - FROMENTINE (Vendée). - La Gare et la Route Nationale de Challans

FROMENTINE — Vue panoramique

This wider view shows how close the station was to the sea. The station building is on the right, and the small loco shed can be seen more clearly. A track runs behind the station building leading to the goods yard.

The track running behind the building can be seen clearly in the bottom picture. The open cabs on the loco's didn't offer much protection to the crews.

FROMENTINE - La Gare

A much more recent picture of the town; the station was alongside the road leading inland on the left.

CHALLANS A FROMENTINE

fr. c.	fr. c.	kil.	(368)				
De Challans			●**Challans-Etat**.dép..	8 32	10 25	16 30	20 45
» 25	» 15	3	Challans-Ville........	8 38	10 30	16 35	20 49
» 55	» 35	7	Les 4 Moul.-Sallertaine	8 56	10 46	16 53	21 5
» 90	» 60	12	St-Gervais-les-Marais ..	9 12	10 59	17 8	21 18
1 20	» 80	16	Beauvoir-sur-Mer......	9 29	11 13	17 24	21 32
1 45	» 95	19	Le Grand-Pont-sur Etier	9 39	11 21	17 33	21 40
1 75	1 15	23	La Barre-de-Monts.....	9 55	11 34	17 48	21 53
1 90	1 25	25	**Fromentine**......arr.	10 »	11 39	17 53	21 58
Corresp.ces pour Noirmoutier			La Fosse ....dép.	10 30	12 10	18 30	...
			Noirmoutier-Ville.arr.	12 »	13 40	20 »	....
Corresp.ces de Noirmoutier			**Noirmoutier**-Ville.dép.	4 45	9 »	12 »	15 45
			La Fosse ....arr.	6 15	10 30	13 30	17 15
fr. c.	fr. c.	kil.					
Fromentine			**Fromentine**......dép.	7 »	11 45	14 25	18 10
» 30	» 20	3	La Barre-de-Monts....	7 6	11 51	14 33	18 16
» 55	» 40	6	Le Grand-Pont-sur Etier	7 19	12 4	14 48	18 29
» 85	» 60	9	Beauvoir-sur-Mer......	7 28	12 13	15 »	18 38
1 20	» 85	13	St-Gervais-les-Marais ..	7 41	12 26	15 15	18 51
1 65	1 20	18	Les 4 Moul.-Sallertaine.	7 54	12 39	15 30	19 4
2 05	1 45	22	Challans-Ville........	8 10	12 55	15 47	19 20
2 30	1 65	25	●**Challans-Etat** ..arr.	8 13	58	15 50	19 28

Arrêts facultatifs : Challans-le-Calvaire, Les Ormeaux, St-Gervais (place de l'Eglise), St-Pie.re.

Le passage du Goulet de Fromentine d'environ 800 mètres de largeur, séparant le Continent (Fromentine) de l'île de Noirmoutier (la Fosse), s'effectue en quelques minutes par un bateau à vapeur très confortable.

Nota. — Les correspondances des trains de Challans à Fromentine avec ceux de l'Etat, ainsi qu'avec les voitures de ou pour Noirmoutier, ne sont indiquées qu'à titre de renseignements et ne sont pas garanties.

CHAPTER 5 NANGIS TO JOUY LE CHATEL

This metre gauge line was another part of the Seine et Marne narrow gauge system but it stands out because it survived until 1965 to serve a Sucrarie and one of the locomotives lasted long enough to be preserved.

The 18km long line was opened in 1901 and was extended to Bray en Seine in 1904. The SM system closed in 1950 but the section form Nangis to Jouy was retained for a further fifteen years purely for the traffic from the Sucarie.

The system was operated using twelve Cail 031 locomotives built in 1901 to which was added a single Buffaud et Robatel 031 in 1904; ironically this is the loco that survives today, no. 3714 which now runs on the Baie de Somme railway.

Nangis has a station on the Paris Est to Mulhouse main line, opened in 1857.

Jouy le Chatel was the centre point of three lines and this is where the sheds and repair shops were located, so I will begin the illustrations there. The intermediate station was at Croix en Brie.

This may have been an important junction between three routes but the station building was still the typical small structure pretty much identical to those at Cayeux & Le Crotoy on the Baie de Somme line. Protection for the passengers was clearly not a priority.

The 'platforms' are simply earth piled slightly higher than the rails. The uneven surface looks decidedly dangerous.

Jouy-le-Châtel — La Gare

Jouy-le-Châtel — Gare

Jouy-le-Châtel — La Gare

The picture below seems to give a fairly accurate impression of what the station looked like.

Jouy-le-Châtel. — La Gare.

The little station of Croix en Brie was the only stopping place between Jouy and Nangis.

The wagon of sugar beet on the loop shows that this was an important traffic right from the start.

La Croix-en-Brie. — L'Arrivée du Train en Gare.

Nangis station ; the Sucrerie was adjacent, and a lot of the workforce probably travelled to the factory by train.

NANGIS (S.-et-M.) — Gare du Tramway de Bray à Sablonnières

832 Nangis — Station du Tramway et Sucrerie

Nangis (S.-et-M.) - La Gare du Tramway

NANGIS (S.-et-M.). - La Gare
C. Bouteille, éditeur, Nangis

The Est Railway station at Nangis….the tramway can be seen running across the foreground of the picture.

A view showing the extent of the sugar factory; the tramway is in the bottom of the picture.

The tramway station is on the left with the goods shed on the right and the lines into the sugar factory in between.

This is what kept the line going; another train loads of sugar beet heads for the factory. This is one of the Cail loco's.

Buffaud et Robatel no. 3714 is seen in 1963, still giving useful service.

Superbly restored, no. 3714 gives us an excellent impression of a train on the tramway to Nangis.

76

CHAPTER 6   RENNES TO PLELAN LE GRAND

This section of the Tramways d'Ille et Vilane was opened in 1898 and was extended to Guer and Redon in 1913. That part closed in 1937 but the original line remained open until 1948. The TIV was an extensive system so here I am going to concentrate on just the line between Rennes and Plelan which passed through stations serving Mordelles, Saint Thurial and Treffendel. I am not going to attempt to cover Rennes itself in detail but I can't resist including some pictures of the wonderful TIV station at the Place de la Mission.

The system had a range of locomotives, opening with Blanc Misserons in 1897 and adding Mallets from Corpet Louvet and smaller 030 tanks from the same makers which were the loco's likely to be seen on the line covered here. Happily no. 75 is preserved in working order, as are some of the TIV coaches.

Railcars were introduced with De Dion Bouton's in 1924, followed in the 1930's by others from Vernez and Billiard. In the era illustrated here though steam was in full command.

This fabulous station was the focal point of the TIV lines in Rennes; lines radiated out from it in all directions as the following postcards show.

90 — RENNES. — Le Mail et la Place de la Mission. J. Sorel, Edit., Rennes.

1275. Rennes. — La Place de la Mission et la Gare des Tramways départementaux

1277. Rennes. — L'Arrivée du Tramway à la Gare de la Place de la Mission

No wonder they could only afford wooden huts at the smaller stations after building this!

88 RENNES (Ille-et-…) Place de la Mission et le Mail. ND. Phot.

2880. Mordelles (I.-et-V.) — La Gare

The first station out of Renens was at Mordelles, another delightful location alongside a row of trees with the village in the background. There is a wagon turntable in front of the station building with a siding at right angles to the running line serving a loading dock seen on the left of the picture.

MORDELLES (I.-et-V.). — L'arrivée de la Gare

The station is just out of the picture on the left.

4171. St-Thurial (I.-et-V.) — Les vallées, passage du Tramway

I haven't found any pictures of St Thurial station so this picture of a freight train in a deep rock cutting near the village will have to suffice.

3773. Treffendel (I.-et-V.) — La Gare et la route de Rennes

Treffendel station was similar to that at Mordelles, with the same wooden station building. The turned finials add an exotic touch to what is really just a wooden shed.

The wagon on the right in the lower picture shows that again a siding was accessed from a wagon turntable, and that may be a goods shed on the far right in which case there may also have been one at Mordelles..

Treffendel (I.-et-V.) — La Gare

The empty landscape does not suggest that this was ever a busy station contributing much to the income of the company.

The only significant settlement on the line was the original terminus at Plelan which had a more impressive brick built station building with a wooden goods shed attached.

PLELAN-LE-GRAND (I.-et-V.). — Les Postes et la Gare.

The locomotive shed on the left of the lower picture would have been built when the station was a terminus; indeed the picture may show it in that condition. The angle of the sidings on the right indicates that again turntables were in use; with narrow gauge wagons this wasn't a problem as they were relatively light. The station building is rather plain and austere.

2876. Plélan-le-Grand (I.-&.-V.) — Vue intérieure de la Gare

La Bretagne Pittoresque
1739. - PLÉLAN-le-GRAND. - La Gare

Collection A. Waron, St-Brieuc

The blinds covering the upper windows would have added a splash of colour.

All the pictures show the Corpet Louvet 030 locomotives which seem to have been used exclusively on the line.

PLÉLAN (I.-et-V.) — La Gare

330 PLÉLAN (Il.-et-V.) - La Gare

Because our only way of picturing these old railways is through the medium of black & white postcards the false impression can be given that they were fairly colourless places...even the hand tinted postcards rarely make any attempt to portray the loco's in anything other than black.

When you look at the preserved No.75 though, you realise that they were anything but colourless.

CHAPTER 7   ST NAZAIRE TO LA ROCHE BERNARD

The CdF du Morbihan was given permission in 1892 to construct a network of metre gauge lines of which the first opened in 1902. More lines were added right up to 1921, but the first closure came in 1935 with the whole system closing in 1947 and 1948, passenger traffic having finished in 1939 despite the introduction of railbuses.

All the steam loco's were 030 tanks, mainly from Pinguely but with three Corpet Louvets added in 1922. Two of the Pinguely tanks are preserved.

St Nazaire was the southernmost extent of the system; the line opened from La Roche Bernard in 1907, the line from Vannes having reached there in 1903. The line lasted until the Second World war; the section from St Nazaire closed in 1943, the remainder lasting until 1847 and 8 when the whole route was closed with the rest of the railway. St Nazaire was seriously damaged during the war and the main line station was pretty much destroyed so it's fair to assume that the adjacent tramway station suffered the same fate.

In this section I am going to cover the terminus at St Nazaire, the intermediate station at St Joachim and finally La Roche Bernard. Herbignac station has been illustrated in a previous volume.

You wonder how they will all get on the train! Holiday crowds at St Naziare tramway station.

From the road, at a higher level than the tracks, it wasn't at all obvious that this was a station so no doubt the large signs on the end walls helped any uncertain travellers.

A wider view shows how close the tramway station was to the rather more imposing main line facilities. This area was virtually destroyed during the Second World War.

In the lower picture the tramway station would have been a short walk along the road to the left.

The tramway station can be seen below the 's' of Nantes.

The small intermediate station at Saint Joachim.

When the line was extended to St Nazaire La Roche Bernard became just another sleepy little through station. A train can be seen approaching on the far left.

21. LA ROCHE-BERNARD (Morbihan) - La Gare

The two road locomotive shed can be seen on the right, provided when the station was a terminus.

Below is my favourite picture of a train on the route so I make no excuse for including it!

10. HERBIGNAC (L.-I.) — Vue générale, prise de la Gare - Arrivée du Train de la Roche-Bernard

One of the three preserved Pinguely 030 locomotives, newly restored.

You might enjoy these other books on French railways:

THE THONES—ANNECY TRAMWAY

THE THIZY TRAMWAY

NARROW GAUGE ON THE ILE DE RE.

NARROW GAUGE INSPIRATION 1

NARROW GAUGE INSPIRATION 2

NARROW GAUGE INSPIRATION 3

And also……

SCRATCHBUILT BUILDINGS THE KIRTLEY WAY

MODELLING SCENERY THE KIRTLEY WAY

STATION COLOURS.

KIRTLEY MODEL BUILDINGS

FOR COMMISSION BUILT LAYOUTS, BUILDINGS & OTHER STRUCTURES, ACCESSORIES, BUILDING PAPERS, BACKSCENE PACKS, INTERIOR KITS & MORE………go to

www.kirtleymodels.com

ALL MAJOR CARDS ACCEPTED

47 KESTREL ROAD MELTON MOWBRAY
LEICS. LE13 0AY   01664 857805
kirtleymodels@ntlworld.com

Printed in Great Britain
by Amazon.co.uk, Ltd.,
Marston Gate.